ERIC ETHAN

Gareth Stevens Publishing
MILWAUKEE

For a free color catalog describing Gareth Stevens Publishing's list of high-quality books and multimedia programs, call 1-800-542-2595 (USA) or 1-800-461-9120 (Canada). Gareth Stevens Publishing's Fax: (414) 225-0377.
See our catalog, too, on the World Wide Web: http://gsinc.com

Library of Congress Cataloging-in-Publication Data

Ethan, Eric.
   GTOs / by Eric Ethan.
     p. cm. — (Great American muscle cars—an imagination library series.
   Includes index.
   Summary: Surveys the history of the GTO and its designs, engines, performance, and costs.
    ISBN 0-8368-1746-X (lib. bdg.)
    1. GTO automobile—Juvenile literature. [1. GTO automobile.]
 I. Title. II. Series: Ethan, Eric. Great American muscle cars—an imagination library series.
 TL215.G79E84 1998
 629.222'2—dc21   97-41187

First published in North America in 1998 by
Gareth Stevens Publishing
1555 North RiverCenter Drive, Suite 201
Milwaukee, WI 53212 USA

This edition © 1998 by Gareth Stevens, Inc. Text by Eric Ethan. Photographs by Ron Kimball (cover, pages 5, 7, 15, and 17) and Nicky Wright (pages 9, 11, 13, 19, and 21). Additional end matter © 1998 by Gareth Stevens, Inc.

Text: Eric Ethan
Page layout: Eric Ethan, Helene Feider
Cover design: Helene Feider
Series design: Shari Tikus

Printed in the United States of America

1 2 3 4 5 6 7 8 9 02 01 00 99 98

TABLE OF CONTENTS

Words that appear in the glossary are printed in **boldface** type the first time they occur in the text.

THE FIRST GTOs

GTOs were built by the Pontiac Motor Company, a division of General Motors, in Pontiac, Michigan. They were the first successful muscle cars of the 1960s. Other carmakers, such as Ford and Chevrolet, followed Pontiac's lead.

The car that started it all almost was not built. In the late 1950s, Pontiacs were not selling well. Pontiac managers at the time — John DeLorean and Simon "Bunkie" Knudson — knew they had to do something in order for the company to survive. They gave Pontiac an exciting new image by creating the GTO. Their plan was risky, but it worked very well — and the **legend** of the GTO was born.

*The GTO was the first successful muscle car of the 1960s. Muscle cars are American-made, two-door sports **coupes** with powerful engines made for high-performance driving. Pictured is a GTO convertible from the first model year in 1964.*

WHAT DO GTOs LOOK LIKE?

In 1963, when DeLorean began to **design** the first GTO, he worked in secret. His bosses at General Motors did not believe the public would buy a high-performance, well-styled car.

DeLorean reworked the design of the Pontiac Tempest. The Tempest was a mid-size car, smaller than the **sedans** other car companies were making. DeLorean gave the Tempest bucket seats, **hood scoops**, and special trim. Most importantly, he gave it a very large engine and the *GTO* name. The GTO had a clean, sporty design and was surprisingly quick. It was exciting to drive. DeLorean believed the car would sell and said *GTO* meant "get those orders."

*After the first couple of years of production, Pontiac engineers redesigned the GTO with a longer **wheelbase**, like this 1968 model.*

WHAT WAS THE FASTEST GTO?

Nearly all GTOs were fast, even the basic models. But many people wanted a more powerful car. They special-ordered larger engines. Pontiac's largest engine was a 389-cubic-inch (6.4-liter) engine with three two-barrel **carburetors**. The greater the cubic inches, the faster the car. The GTO could go faster than the Corvette, Chevrolet's lightweight sports car. It could even keep up with foreign-made sports cars like the Ferrari.

Pontiac couldn't build enough of the 1964 high-performance GTOs to meet demand. The 389 horsepower **tripower** GTO was a remarkable car. Designed in secret in just over six months, it was the fastest muscle car of the 1960s.

The 1965 GTO with a 389-cubic-inch (6.4-liter) engine.

GTO ENGINES

In 1964 and 1965, GTOs were mid-size cars. The Tempest that GTOs were based on originally came with a small four-**cylinder** motor. So when a large eight-cylinder motor was placed into a GTO's small engine **compartment**, it was a tight fit.

The 389-horsepower V-8 was the biggest engine offered in the GTO. The Rochester tripower carburetor setup made it very powerful. Carburetors mix air and gasoline. Three carburetors allow the engine to take in much more air and gasoline than just one, so the engine can run faster.

The 389-cubic-inch (6.4-liter) GTO engine featured three two-barreled carburetors visible at the top of the engine.

GTO INTERIORS

Tempests in the early 1960s had very few interior **options**, such as bucket seats, and the price was low. The GTO was a sportier car and more expensive.

Bucket seats were standard in the GTO. When the car **accelerated** quickly, passengers could hold onto a grab bar located in front of the seat. The GTO also had special gauges in the center of the dashboard to indicate how the high-performance engine was operating. Between the bucket seats was a **stick shift** to operate the car's manual **transmission**. (Most sedans at the time had automatic transmissions.) Just to the left of the grab bar was the special GTO logo.

The interior of this 1965 GTO tripower came with all the usual muscle car equipment of the era, including a stick shift, bucket seats, and special gauges.

GTOs RACING

The GTO was built to go fast on the straightaway. It did not handle corners well. **Drag racing** was popular with GTO owners. In drag racing, two cars race against each other down a straight quarter-mile course. Legal drag racing was organized by the National Hot Rod Association. In the early 1960s, it became one of America's largest spectator sports.

Drag racing showcased the GTO's best qualities — rapid acceleration and high top speed. A GTO could reach up to 105 miles (170 kilometers) per hour and cover the quarter mile in just thirteen seconds. Drag racing on official racetracks is safe, fun, and legal. It is very dangerous to drag race on city streets, and responsible drivers never do this.

In 1969, Pontiac released a special version of the GTO called the "Judge," named after a popular comedy character.

15

BEAUTIFUL GTOs

Many people believe the 1965 GTO convertible is the most beautiful car ever made. For that model year, the GTO underwent major changes in body styling. The headlights were stacked one on top of another, instead of side-by-side as they were earlier. The grill was split into two parts. These and other style changes made the GTO an enormous success in its first years of production.

In the years after 1965, GTOs grew larger, and the design changed even more. Although the later cars sold well, they were never as popular as the 1965 models.

Many fans of the GTO believe the 1965 model, like the convertible pictured, combined the best elements of high performance and design.

THE LAST GTOs

The last GTO was made in 1974. By that time, concerns about pollution and increased gasoline prices made high-performance cars less popular. And, for safety reasons, government regulations placed limits on what carmakers could offer in powerful cars.

By 1970, GTOs looked almost nothing like they did in 1965. The 1970 GTO model, the "Judge," was a high-performance luxury car. The model was not popular. But by 1970, the end of the muscle car era was in sight. People who designed and built the GTO were very proud of their car. They decided in 1974 to stop making them because they could no longer build them the way they wanted to.

The 1970 Judge was one of the last high-performance GTOs.

WHAT DID ORIGINAL GTOs COST?

During the 1960s, most new sedans cost less than $5,000. The mid-size Tempest that the GTO was based on cost even less. Options increased the price of a new car. But even with a larger engine and special interior features, car prices usually did not top $5,000.

Today, most new cars cost two or three times that amount. GTOs manufactured between 1964 and 1967 were real bargains even at the time.

*This beautifully **restored** Pontiac GTO cost less than $5,000 when it was originally made in 1965.*

WHAT DO GTOs COST TODAY?

Between 1969 and 1974, almost 63,000 GTO convertibles were made. Today, less than 10,000 exist. Only a few of those survivors are in good condition. GTOs with the V-8 and tripower carburetor option were manufactured in smaller numbers. Very few of these models can be found today.

Scarcity increases the value of muscle cars from the 1960s that are in good condition. Cars that cost less than $5,000 when new are worth almost $25,000 today. Collectors are willing to pay more for well-maintained, all-original cars. Most collectors see their GTOs as more than just a good investment. To them, the GTO is a classic example of the heavy metal wonder cars of a time gone by.

GLOSSARY

accelerated (ek-SELL-er-ay-ted) — Greatly increased speed.

carburetor (CAR-burr-ay-ter) — The part of a car that supplies the engine with an explosive, vaporized fuel-air mixture.

compartment (kom-PART-ment) — A separate area surrounded by four walls or sides.

coupe (koop) — An enclosed, two-door automobile that is smaller than a sedan.

cylinder (SILL-in-der) — The tube-shaped piston chamber in an engine.

design (dee-ZINE) — The plans and specifications for a new product.

drag racing (DRAG rase-ing) — An acceleration contest between cars that travel in a straight line over a quarter-mile course.

hood scoop — The part of a car that brings fresh air into the engine compartment.

legend (LEJ-end) — Something that is very well known or famous.

option (OP-shun) — A feature that can be added over and above standard features.

restore (ree-STORE) — To fix an item so that it becomes like new.

sedan (seh-DAN) — A large, enclosed automobile that can seat six adults. It has a front and rear seat.

stick shift (STIHK shift) — A manually operated gearshift that is mounted on the steering column or floor of an automobile.

transmission (trans-MIH-shun) — The part of a car that transfers the engine's power to the axles.

tripower (TRY POW-er) — The presence of three carburetors on an engine, instead of the standard one.

wheelbase (WEEL-base) — The distance between the front and rear axles of an automobile.

WEB SITES

www.pontiac.com/

trantor.cse.psu.edu/~croberts/rc.html

members.iquest.net/~mattingly/6869goat.htm

www.owt.com/users/waltsch/pontiac

PLACES TO WRITE

High Performance Pontiac
  McMullen and Argus Publishing
  774 South Placentia Avenue
  Placentia, CA 92870-6832

GTO Association of America
  5829 Stroebel Road
  Saginaw, MI 48609
  1-800-GTO-1964

Classic Motorbooks
  729 Prospect Avenue, P.O. Box 1
  Osceola, WI 54020
  1-800-826-6600

Pontiac Enthusiast
  P.O. Box 6489
  Orange, CA 92613-6489

INDEX